I0541844

$5K THE WRITE WAY

PROVEN METHODS TO GENERATE $5K FROM YOUR BOOK

TIMOTHY O. BOND

TrueVinePublishing.org

$5k The Write Way
Timothy O. Bond

Published by True Vine Publishing Co.
810 Dominican Dr. Ste 103
Nashville, TN 37228
www.TrueVinePublishing.org

Copyright © 2023 by Timothy O. Bond

Copyright Disclaimer:

All rights reserved. No part of this book may be reproduced in any form or by any electronic or mechanical means, including information storage and retrieval or mechanical means without permission in writing from the publisher, except by a reviewer who may quote brief passages **in a review.**

ISBN: 978-1-956469-66-0 Paperback
ISBN: 978-1-956469-67-7 eBook

Printed in the United States—first printing

TABLE OF CONTENTS

INTRODUCTION:

Congratulations!

If you're reading this book then you are on a path that can lead to unlimited wealth, freedom, and fulfillment. However, it will not happen the way most people think. The average person believes writing a book will make them wealthy just by the sheer nature of writing the book. However, this is the same mindset that leads to 95% of books published being unprofitable.

In this book, we're going to discuss how to make $5,000 with your book, but I believe once you have learned the system, all you'll need to do is Rinse, Repeat, and Increase. Your $5K activities, doubled, will lead to $10k. Triple those activities, and technically, you should generate $15k. But then, God has instilled a nice little bonus for those who prove that they are serious about succeeding. He adds compound interest. Your one customer tells her friends about you and multiplies your results. 2+2 no longer equals 4, it can equal 1000.

I want to provide you with the fundamentals of bookselling. It's not pretty, and it's not easy, but it's reality. This is not a something-for-nothing concept. There is no way to override universal laws. The law states that you reap what you sow. No one gets a harvest without planting seeds, and no one gets a harvest with passive action. You have to work for success and your book is no different. If you work a job, go to your boss and ask him or her if you can still get paid full-time wages while only working one hour per week.

After you've been laughed out of the office, consider this: if you're willing to work 40 hours per week to make your employer's vision successful, why are you looking for a way to avoid working to make your own vision a success?

In this book, you will find your success in three areas:

Mind: All success begins in the mind. You don't see money with your eyes, you must first see it with your mind. Until you believe you can achieve your goals without an inkling of doubt, you will never achieve them.

Planning: Once you have set your mind on your goal, the next step is to start planning. A goal without a plan is just a daydream. The cliche that people should chase their dreams is a bunch of hogwash. I say, "Stop chasing your dream and start following your vision." Dreams end when you open your eyes. When people open their eyes to the realities of what it takes to achieve their dreams, the majority, 97% in fact, close their eyes and go back to sleep. However, vision only ends when you close your eyes. The person who will keep their eyes open, create a plan and simply follow each step, will inevitably achieve success.

Execution: Don't talk about it, be about it. Everything we see in this world is the result of execution. Your home was an imagination of an architect. Your job was once the founder's dream. The outfit you are wearing today was an idea in your head this morning that you had to execute. You don't have to execute 100% perfectly every time, but you *must* execute. You may find errors, typos, or misspelled words in this book, but you are reading the book because of execution. The information you get in this book and my master-class means nothing if you do not execute.

I hope you'll find great value in this book, but above all, I hope that you will EXECUTE.

Fair warning: I believe a good coach challenges you to be something better. That challenge may, at times, offend some. In this book, I'll use the word "you". Please don't take it personally. If the information hurts, that's a good sign that your nerves are still alive and ready to heal and grow. If you don't feel any emotion from these words, we may need to perform CPR.

MIND

EVERYTHING STARTS WITHIN YOUR OWN MIND. YOUR THOUGHTS, ATTITUDE AND DETERMINATION ARE ALL ESSENTIAL FOR SUCCESS. GYMQUOTES.CO

CHAPTER 1

DECIDE

"There is a redemptive power that making a choice has, rather than feeling like you're an effect to all the things that are happening. Make a choice. Just decide what it's going to be, who you're going to be, how you're going to do it. Just decide. And then from that point, the universe is going to get out of your way... I feel very strongly, that we are who we choose to be."

−Will Smith

The first and most important step to succeeding in anything is deciding to succeed. Your future is yours to shape. Life does not happen to you. Life happens through you. Until you believe that, you will always be searching for a hand up, looking for that "big break" or waiting for Oprah to find your book.

You have the power to write your story like an author writing a novel. And the great thing is, you are the main character, so you get to make yourself the rich and wealthy hero. So make the decision.

Making a decision empowers you in three major ways.

First, making a decision is an invitation to the Universe (God) to engage in your mission. The Bible states a double minded man is unstable in all his ways. Let not that man think he shall receive anything from God. You have to make a definitive choice about what you want out of your life, and your commitment to obtain it no matter what price, consequence, or sacrifice you'll have to make. When you do that, you will attract and magnetize the resources, people, and opportunities you need.

Second, making a decision activates your awareness. Most of us walk around blind to the opportunities and resources to achieve our dreams. They are sitting right under our noses but because we are not aware of what we want, we can't see them. When you make a decision, your eyes will be opened to the opportunities to make your decision a reality.

When you decide to sell 100 books in seven days, you see people differently. The people you see reading books in the office look like customers now. Your high school buddy who is a radio disc jockey now looks like a great opportunity to promote your book.

Lastly, making a decision brings about self-accountability. I'm a serial procrastinator. But when I've made a definitive decision, the voice in my head that usually tries to talk me out of discomfort becomes a source of discomfort when I'm not moving toward my objective. I become more accountable to myself when I've made a decision.

Decide how much money you want to make from your book?

Most authors write books and are excited *to see* how much money they will make. The problem with this mindset is that the author places themselves in a dependent state, relying on the fickle pleasures of the market.

You should decide how much money you want to make. Don't leave it up to others and wait to see who buys your book. Decide how much money you need to make and then go out and make the market acquiesce to your demand.

My decision:

Today, _____,

I decide to make $_____ from my

book in a _____month period.

CHAPTER 2

ADOPT THE PRO MENTALITY

I have been publishing books for 19 years as of this month. For 16 of those years, I published books as a hobby. In 2020, God snatched the training wheels off of my career and told me, it's time for you to go pro. Since that day on September 19, 2020, I have generated more money from my business than ever.

What stopped me from making this kind of money 16 years ago? I'd venture to say, I didn't have the pro mentality. I didn't see my business as my profession, so I didn't put the effort, energy, sacrifice, and investments into the business that I should have.

Now that you have written your book, do you see yourself as a pro, or was this just a good idea that you hope will sprout wings and fly to the highest heights?

As an author, you must understand that you are a business. The moment you sell your first book, Uncle Sam declares you a business and he is not joking. So you should not joke around either.

A pro mentality works the business: Professional athletes don't send friends to the gym to work out on their behalf. Professional real estate agents don't sit at home waiting for new clients to knock on the door, and professional authors don't hand off their success to third parties.

Your publisher is not responsible for your success. Putting your book on Amazon is like putting your needle in a haystack. Amazon is not actively telling people about your individual book. If you searched a book title on Amazon and looked at the bottom of the page, you may find there are 200 pages of options.

A professional understands that no one can make their book successful but themselves. They have to put forth the effort and energy to achieve their goals. This doesn't mean they can't get help, but that help must lead back to the author showing his or her face and pitching his/her product.

A Pro mentality promotes the business: Most authors try to avoid promoting. They fear rejection. They think their book is their baby and rejection of the book is a rejection of their baby. Stop it! A pro mentality understands that the only way anyone is going to know that the book exists is by promoting it. You have to tell people about the book in any and every way. Social media, podcasting, interviews, passing out business cards and postcards, car magnets, the list goes on.

A Pro mentality Invests in the business: Investment comes in many forms: Investments of money, time, energy, and resources. To achieve success as an author, you must invest in yourself. Invest the money it takes to market and promote your book. You can't reach everyone. You need to pay people, organizations, platforms who can reach more people.

Energy: I know you're tired after a long day's work, but you have to find some energy to promote and sell your book. Even if you're sitting on the couch eating popcorn, take some time to talk to your audience and promote your book.

Hire help: Invest in people and resources who can help spread the word. Offer commissions. Sure, you may make a little less money, but **a little less of something is better than all of nothing.**

Adopting a pro mentality means you take this book seriously. You see this as a career, your future, and your legacy to pass down. If you're resistant to the notion of investing time, energy, and money into your book, then you can't expect the same results as someone who does. No, you don't have to quit your job to be successful. If your book is a side gig, then you simply must be okay with side gig money.

Note: There are programs that offer massive exposure and book sales for little to nothing. Think about these services like fast food. If a restaurant is offering 5 double cheeseburgers, 6 chicken nuggets, and large fries for $.99, you have to ask yourself what the food is made of because it's too cheap to be real food.

CHAPTER 3

ACTIVATE YOUR FIGHT MODE

How do you trigger motivation? We've all heard of the "fight or flight" response. These are the two instinctive responses humans have to danger. They will either run away from it, or they will stand and fight it. Did you know that the same chemicals that trigger a man to run from a grizzly bear are the same chemicals that will trigger you to run from promoting your book?

Think about that. In your brain, asking someone to buy your book is just as threatening as a grizzly bear charging to eat you. But here's the thing: it's not the same, and you know it's not the same.

You have to take control of these emotions and find a way to activate your Fight Mode. Motivation is not a lightning bolt that can only hit you when you're standing in the right spot. Motivation is something that you can manipulate and use as a tool.

Michael Jordan and LaBradford Smith

There's a great story about Michael Jordan and LaBradford Smith who played for the Washington Bullets. Smith had a great game, scoring 36 points and beating the Bulls in a playoff game. After the game, Michael Jordan told his teammates that LaBradford walked up and put his arm around his shoulder, and said, sarcastically, "Good game Mike." Jordan told his team that he was going to make LaBradford pay for this in the next game. He told his team that he was going to score 36 points on LaBradford in the first quarter to make him eat his words.

In Jordan fashion, Michael did exactly what he said he would do. He dominated the next game, scoring 36 points in the first half and defeating the Bullets. Years later, a rumor was going around that Jordan lied about the sarcastic exchange. When a reporter asked Jordan, "is it true that the incident with LaBradford Smith never happened?" Jordan laughed and confessed, "No, he never did that."

Jordan created a false offense in order to dominate his opponent.

What do you need to fight and dominate your goal?

I have come to learn that I am most activated when my back is against the wall. As a life-long procrastinator, I realized that I get a high from achieving something at the last minute. My good friend and business coach, Adrian Davis, helped me realize that I'm addicted to the adrenaline rush. So I decided to use this knowledge to my benefit.

Since I know what triggers my fight mode, I create situations that require me to fight. I set short-term goals that require manic, aggressive action to achieve. For the last quarter of 2022, I set a goal to publish 30 books. Publishing 30 books in three months meant I needed to find and sign 10 authors a month. To do that, I knew I needed to be active daily.

To achieve my goal, I had to obliterate my comfort zone. I conducted daily IG live interviews, something I was terrified of doing. I made myself accountable to the world of social media by posting every new contract I procured. I called old clients and jumped into people's DMs. Did I achieve my goal? NO. But I did get 15 new clients, generating a little under $70k in new business in that 3-month period. Do you think I was upset?

What does it take for you to go into Fight Mode? Does the thought of being embarrassed drive you crazy? Then tell everyone about your goal and then fight like hell not to be embarrassed.

When your back is against the wall and you trigger your fight mode, you don't care what people

think, you don't care if you are swinging perfectly, you don't care how little sleep you have
gotten or how much food you have eaten. You
don't care if you're coming across as pushy or if
people think you're corny. The only thing that
matters is getting your back off of that wall.

Create a goal that you can't stomach the thought
of not achieving. That's not to say you will 100%
achieve the goal. If it's too easy to achieve then
it's not a good goal. Create a goal wherein even
failure would make you more successful than
you were before.

What is your fight mode trigger?

_____

_____

_____

_____

_____

_____

_____

_____

_____

_____

_____

_____

_____

_____

_____

_____

_____

_____

_____

_____

_____

_____

DEVELOP YOUR PLAN

> By failing to **prepare**, you are preparing to fail.
>
> – Benjamin Franklin

CHAPTER 4

CREATE THE DREAM BUT CHASE THE VISION

Creating the Dream:

Many people don't know how to create a vision for their books. However, they don't realize that they already have the vision, they just don't recognize it as a vision. To them, it's just a daydream. Fancies of sitting at a table signing books to a long line of fans. They imagine themselves being interviewed at a radio station or on the news. They see themselves standing before a group of people talking about their books.

These "daydreams" are actually the building blocks of success. Daydreams are your imagination at work, and your imagination is actually a quantum leap into a realm where you have the opportunity to create the future.

As I said before, everything we see is the product of someone's imagination. Amazon was Jeff Bezos's imagination that he could use the internet as a means of commerce. He took that daydream and chose books as his pilot product because his research showed books are the most purchased product in the world. Bezos's imagination has changed the way the world is shaped.

You are no different. You too can create your dream of what success as an author looks like for you. Simply take five to 10 minutes to dream. Close your eyes now and answer these questions. Don't qualify or quantify what you see. Just write it down. I had one client do this exercise and she told me "for some reason, I see myself in the airport." I felt that was a powerful moment.

She felt it was a strange idea, but I believe she was viewing the future.

What do you see when you think about selling books: Where are you? Who's there? What's the energy of the room?

_____

_____

_____

_____

Where do you see yourself promoting your books?

_____

_____

_____

_____

Where are you as you speak to groups of people about your book?

_____

_____

_____

_____

What does your website look like?

_____

_____

_____

_____

You're in a networking event and someone asks what your book is about. What do you tell them?

_____

_____

_____

_____

Chasing the Vision:

Now that you have the dream, it's time to create the vision to make it a reality. But first, take some more time to dream about every aspect of your being a successful author. Think about everything you want. How many people are working for you? How much money are you ultimately making? Where are you vacationing? What kind of car are you driving? Everything!

After you have written out the dream, create the plan by reverse engineering the dream.

(Note: Understand that by writing down your dream, you have made it a tangible reality. It now exists in the universe as a physical thing. And if it is a physical thing, it can now be manifested.)

Write down every step of achieving that dream in detail. Take into account the clothes you are wearing, the money you will make, the designs and decorations. Create your reality. The plan doesn't even need to be sound. You can always adapt the plan as you learn, but until you create the plan, you'll never start.

Here's an example of reverse engineering your dream into a Vision:

I see myself being interviewed on different podcasts.
Step 1: Research all of the podcasters who reach my target audience

Step 2: Create a list of all the podcasts I want to be interviewed on.

Step 3: Reach out to the podcast host and find out what it takes to be a guest on their show.

Step 4: Comply with all of the requirements to be a guest on the show

Step 5: Develop my speaking points

Step 6: Be a guest on the show.

(Note: You can hire people to do this for you. Remember your pro mentality. Being committed doesn't mean you have to do everything.)

I see myself conducting a book signing at Barnes & Noble.

- Step 1: Contact Barnes & Noble to find out what I need to do to host a book signing
- Step 2: Create budget
- Step 3: Create marketing material to promote my book signing
- Step 4: Create a t-shirt with my book on the front
- Step 5: Get some standing banners designed and printed.

- Step 6: Buy a branded tablecloth and a bowl for candy.
- Step 7: Come up with some icebreakers, games, and incentives to keep people engaged.
- Step 8: Enlist the people who will help me during the signing.
- Step 9: Set a date
- Step 10: Conduct the following promotional activities every day until the event
- Step 11: Host my book signing at the _____ location Barnes & Noble

One step at a time:

I have heard this old adage all my life, but as a businessman, I truly appreciate it now. A journey of 1000 miles begins with the first step. So many people stop short of achieving greatness because they can't see through the fog of uncertainty. Because they don't know what lies ahead, they don't even take a step in the direction of their greatness.

Success is nothing more than a series of executed steps. The saying goes "no one can stop a man with a plan because no one has a plan to stop him." If you create a plan, simply take one step at a time. Don't try to see every twist and turn, valley and peak. Just take one step. Yes, you may have obstacles that may cause you to stop and rethink your next step, or adjust your footing, but it won't stop you from making the step.

You have to believe that your vision is appointed and approved by God and God is with you. You can't fail if you don't give up. If you decide to walk from your bedroom to your kitchen, you will get there if you just keep walking. Success is no different.

Take it one step at a time. You've already set your sights on where you want to go, so just take the steps you planned.

$$W = \frac{1}{2\mu_0}\left[\frac{\Psi'^2\pi^2}{b^2}\sum_{m,n}a_{mn}^2 n^2(ab/4) + \frac{\Psi'^2\pi^2}{a^2}\sum_{m,n}a_{mn}^2 m^2(ab/4)\right.$$

$$\left. + \Psi'^2 ab\left(\mu^2 + \sum_{m,n}\frac{8a_{mn}\mu^2}{\pi^2 mn} + \frac{a_{mn}^2\mu^2}{4}\right)\right]$$

$$W = \frac{\Psi'^2 ab}{2\mu_0}\left[\mu^2 + \sum_{m,n}\left(\frac{a_{mn}^2}{4}\left(\frac{m^2\pi^2}{a^2} + \frac{n^2\pi^2}{b^2} + \mu^2\right) + \frac{8a_{mn}\mu^2}{\pi^2 mn}\right)\right]. \qquad (1)$$

CHAPTER 5

THE SUCCESS EQUATION

Deciding how much money you want to make and how many books you want to sell is actually quite simple. When you finish this chapter, you'll probably say, "Well, duh."

How much money do you want to make?
I know your first thought may be "A MILLION DOLLARS!" Everyone wants to be a millionaire, I get it. But if you don't currently make $1 million dollars per year, it is because of this reason... Get ready... It's *because you're not a millionaire*.

You have to *become* a millionaire before you can become a millionaire. You make money in direct correlation to the type of person you are. This does not mean you can't become a millionaire. You can grow to become a millionaire by learning, planning, and executing the things millionaires do. When you become that person, then the money will come by default.

Getting back to the point. If you're not a millionaire, then don't expect to make $1 million from your book right away. Instead, set goals in line with the person you are. However, make these goals stretch you to become something greater.

Set a goal for compounding growth. Instead of setting some obscure number, think about how much you would like to increase your current income in a 12 month period. For example, if you make $50,000 per year, then perhaps you'd like to set a goal to increase your income with your book by 20%. Thus, your income goal would be $10,000.

(Note: If 20% is an easy task, then set a percentage that will push you out of your comfort zone. A goal that will force you to do things you'd not

usually do, go places you'd usually not go, and meet people you'd usually not meet.)

When you achieve your goal, the next year, use that same strategy and increase your book income to 20% of $60,000. Within 2 years, you will have gone from $50,000 to $72,000.

Remember what I said before about God's bonus?

(Note: If you think these numbers are unambitious, think again. 95% of books fail to earn $5,000, and the majority of non-ficton books in America fail to sell more than 250 copies. Creating a system that increases your income by 20% is spectacular.)

How many books do you want to sell?

Many authors are stomped when I ask this question because they are stuck in the dependency mindset. They believe their book sales depend on who wants to buy the book. But that is wrong.

The number of books depends on your determination not to stop until you hit that number.

Your number of book sales is actually tied to your monetary goals. This exercise will show you exactly how many books you need to sell.

Success is achieved in consistent, incremental gains.

Fill in the Information as Follows: (Note: I'll leave the blanks open for you to fill in your own numbers.)

I'm GOING to earn (Earnings)
$_____ in _____ months

The retail price of my book is $_____

My Earnings divided by my retail price
$_____ / $_____ = _____(books)
Books divided by # of months
____(bks)/ ____(mos)= _____(sales per month)

Sales per month divided by 4

_____(spm)/4 = _____(sales per week)

Sales per week divided by 7

_____(spw)/7 = _____ (sales per day)

Based on this equation: Your goal of selling $5,000 worth of books in 3 months, would look like this:

I'm going to earn $5,000   in   3 months

My retail price is $ 15

My earnings divided by my retail price
$5,000 / $15   = 333.3 books

Books divide by # of months
333 / 3   = 111 sales per month

Sales per month divided by 4
111 / 4 = 27.75 sales per week

Sales per week divided by 7

27.75/ 7 = 4 per day

There's the goal. **4 books per day.** How many people do you run into, meet, and interact with per day? Do an experiment and keep a tab of every person you talk to today. Even the people you pass in the grocery store and smile at. These are all potential buyers. And as a person with a "Pro mentality," you don't let potential buyers walk away without at least offering them your product.

CHAPTER 6

TARGETING YOUR CUSTOMERS

Okay, you have the mentality to succeed. You've decided that you want to be successful, and how much money you want to make. You have activated your Fight Mode. You see the dream and have written out the vision (plan). Now it's time to find your readers.

This is where rubber meets the road. To achieve your monetary goals ($5k for the purpose of this book) you now have to find your buyers. They are not going to come to you. You have to go to them. Don't leave it to chance. Target your buyers. You don't have to know them, but it helps.

Your goal should be to find a guaranteed way to make your money. When a Lion stalks it's prey, it doesn't just charge the pack. They study their prey to find the sick, old and babies. Time and energy are of the essence.

Likewise, you'll do yourself a great service by making sure that you study and pick your readers for the easiest sale. We'll discuss how to make this job easier.

Three easy targets

First target: Your personal circle of influence. Who do you know who will support you simply because your name is on the book? Create a list of your top 100-200 supporters. This includes family, friends, church members, fellow social club, fraternity and sorority members, and even grade school classmates.

Check your phone. How many numbers do you have in it? These are all potential buyers. Check your email contacts. How many emails do you have? These too are potential buyers. Typically when I suggest this, people create self-imposed boundaries as to why they can't reach out to these people.

"No, those are co-workers, I can't call them about my book."
"No, you don't know my family. My family is weird."

All I hear is "I'm afraid of being rejected by people I know."

If you want to succeed at your goals, you can't do it by ruling out the things you're uncomfortable with. The most successful people in this life have found that it's better to beg pardon than to beg permission. In most cases, for every one person who takes offense at your ambition, 10 people will applaud and supported it.

2nd Target: Your Target Market

Your next easy target is the person for whom you wrote the book. If I was a business coach, I'd be talking to you about identifying your target customer. But let's make it simple by answering this question:

What problem does your book solve and who has that problem? Every book, even novels have some kind of value that can be marketed to a particular group. Your goal is to find thousands of people in your target market. I'm sorry, millions. Once you have identified your target market, now, you need to find out where they are. Where are they hanging out? With whom do they network? What magazines or newspapers do they read? What television shows do they watch? What social media groups are they in? After finding your target market, your next challenge will be effectively attracting them to take action.

What problem does my book solve?

_____

_____

_____

_____

Who has that problem?

_____   _____

_____   _____

_____   _____

Where Are They Hanging Out?

_____   _____

_____   _____

_____   _____

With whom do they network?

_____   _____

_____   _____

_____   _____

What magazines, websites, newspapers, podcasts, television shows do they read and watch?

_____   _____

_____   _____

_____   _____

What social media groups are they in?

_____   _____

_____   _____

_____   _____

Third target: Referrals

Word of mouth is still the best marketing resource. People do business with people they trust, and with those who are referred by someone they trust. Your current customers are a great source for new customers. You just need to engage them. If you have customers who are happy with your product, they will happily send more business your way. Ask for the referral. The worse they can say is "they don't know anyone." No harm, no foul. But the one person you get who gives you a valid referral was worth every "No" you received.

CHAPTER 7

GENERATE LEADS

Getting people to buy your book is no different than getting people to buy cars, real estate, or counseling. You have to attract them with something that they want, and in return, you get an opportunity to offer your product. There is no magic wand that makes people telepathically aware of your book. People buy products that will benefit them in some way, shape, or form. It can be entertainment, it can be education, therapy, or self-development.

Host training sessions (webinars/ workshops): One of the best ways to generate leads is to

50

speak to groups. There is no getting around it. When I speak at events, I get new clients. If you have a non-fiction book, then you have the potential to host webinars, coaching sessions, and other events to share valuable knowledge. That knowledge will lead to more sales.

If you have a fiction book, you still have the same opportunity to host book-reading parties, and novel-writing classes, and provide other valuable resources for people to learn more about you and your book.

Be A Vendor at mass-populated events: Book fairs, county fairs, conferences. These are all great opportunities to become a vendor and set up a table for exposure, more leads, more prospects, and more customers. You have to go to where your readers are. You can't sit at home waiting for book sales to come to you.

Networking Events: Are you an active member of your corporate community? Do people know your face and name? It has been said that your net worth is tied to your network. Get out and hang with the movers and shakers in your business community. Make friends. Don't go to network events looking to pitch your business. Go to network events to make new relationships. People support people they like but they refer people they trust.

It's a numbers game: When it comes down to it, you need to be in front of more people.

CHAPTER 8

DATA IS THE NEW GOLD

Your greatest asset as an author is your list of names and contacts– your database.

Your database of buyers, inquirers, and supporters are worth its weight in gold. In Kevin Hart's Book, *Don't F**K This Up,* Kevin explains how he rose to the megastar he is today. Kevin explains that he decided to start collecting contact information at all of his shows. He began sending out emails and tweets about his upcoming shows and events. He said that sometimes there would be small crowds, but even in the small crowds he was happy if his database grew by one new name. Kevin Hart turned his database into a multimillion fan base. He financed his first special and sold out based on the power of his database. That show catapulted him to the mogul he has become.

Don't give your database away. Your number one goal as a business is to make money and to do that, you need customers.

1. Create a spreadsheet
2. Insert every name in your phone and on your email list.
3. Wherever you go, your job is to collect names or money.
4. Maintain consistent contact with your database. Send a regular newsletter, product updates, upcoming events, and helpful information.

Name	Email	Phone	Mailing Address	Social media

CHAPTER 9

ASK!

When you get in front of more people, make the ask! You do yourself a disservice by not asking people to buy your book or service. 9 times out of 10, you're not getting the results you want, simply because you're not asking. I can't tell you how many authors I follow on social media whose page is filled with selfies, pictures of food, and clothes but not one video or picture about their book.

Even sadder are the authors who have platforms that don't promote their books on their own platforms. I've seen authors speak to hundreds of people and walk out without acknowledging their books. Even worse, they didn't even have books on them. I've been to events hosted by authors where the author did not promote their own book.

Create Your Sales Pitch: It's important that when you get someone to talk to, you have something of quality to say. You must create a strong sales pitch detailing what your book is about and how it benefits your readers. If you are meandering through a 20-minute conversation about your book, you're wasting time, energy, and opportunities. You need a 30-second elevator pitch that will compel your lead to take action.

Don't stop until you get a Yes or No.

When your leads become prospects, don't stop asking for the sale until you get the money in your hand or they tell you "NO! Leave me alone!" A pro mentality closes the deal. Most people have to be reminded 7 to 15 times to take action. Also, you never know what a person is going through at any given point. Just because someone disappears does not mean they are saying no.

It is your responsibility to make the sale, not to worry about how people feel about your approach. If they don't like you, they represent one person in a world of 7 billion. Keep going.

Points of Contact:

When you create your list of targets, you need to contact them in every possible way.

Phone: Let people hear your voice and personality. Utilize calling apps that allow you to send mass phone messages. When I executed my presale campaign, I sent out 100 messages at 5:00 p.m. with the push of a button.

Text: After you have made the phone call, then engage in texting. Also, use apps that allow you to send mass text messages. There are CRM programs that will trigger automated phone calls and text messages.

Email: Utilize apps like MailChimp for mass emails and drip campaigns.

Mailing Address: Send physical paper mail. Postcards, sales letters, follow-up letters. People communicate best in different ways. Offer them all.

Social Media Direct messaging: Utilize social media. LinkedIn provides special access to contacting professionals for $75

Face-to-Face: If you have to go knock on doors, meet at offices, or take someone out to lunch, make the sale.

EXECUTE

CHAPTER 10

EXECUTION

"No excuses. No explanation. You don't win on emotion. You win on execution."

—Tony Dungy

None of this matters if you don't execute. You don't have to execute everything you have learned in the next 24 hours either. Like a baby, take one step at a time. As long as you are consistent, you will continue to grow and expand.

When I reboot my workout regimens, I always start with a simple but effective machine—the elliptical machine. I commit to working out on the elliptical machine every day. As my heart health and muscle memory improve, I push myself to do more. I decide to go running. Then I decide to start lifting weights. One improvement leads to another. Your exposure and sales will grow as you execute one new discipline at a time. There is no rush on success. If you are making progressive moves, then you're doing the right thing.

However, don't play yourself. This is not an excuse to do less than you are capable of doing. You couldn't stay in the first grade after you mastered the material, because there were higher levels of growth. Likewise, you can't just do the things you're good at. Yes, you've gotten comfortable with posting on social media, but now you have to go live with no editing ability. You have to continue to push yourself to execute at a higher level.

Here are three helpful tips for mastering execution.

Do it afraid: We all have a voice in our heads that tells us that we are not equipped, prepared, or even worthy of the success we seek. That voice is a liar. Remember your ability to quantum leap into the future, come back, and create your reality. You do it every day. Creating your vision for success is no different. Even though you are afraid, just take the simple steps you laid out to reach the end result. Don't look at the obstacles. Don't listen to the naysayers. Just follow the yellow-brick road.

"I Don't Care": A trick that I use to push myself to execute is to say out loud, "I Don't Care." When I pursue huge goals, I tend to start thinking of the worse possible outcomes. To shut that voice up, I say "I don't care" out loud. I don't care if no one comes. I don't care if people don't like it. I don't care if I lose money. Then, I replace those thoughts with the benefits I will enjoy. "I will improve my public speaking skills." "I will learn from my experience to do it better next time." "I'll have good video footage to post on Instagram."

Don't concern yourself with the negatives that will happen. So what! You will receive far more benefits from your execution, than consequences.

Build your team: It has been said there is no best-selling author, there's only a best-selling team. There is boldness in numbers. I can do some really bold and audacious stunts when I'm with my business partner. Just knowing that someone has my back and will pick me up if I fall takes away the fear. Who is on your success team? Draw energy, boldness, and creativity from each other.

Members who should be on your Execution Team:

1. Coach
2. Accountability team
3. Sales Support
4. Someone who is good at marketing and promotion
5. An assistant to handle low-value activities (any activities that don't generate money)
6. Graphic designer

Add to your list

_____   _____

_____   _____

_____   _____

_____   _____

_____   _____

_____   _____

_____   _____

_____   _____

_____   _____

YOUR $5K PLAN

Step 1: Set a specific date

Having a deadline is critical for a few reasons. First, it activates your Fight Mode. Your back is against the wall. You must succeed. Secondly, it allows you to quantify your progress. You can set a monetary goal for every day, week, and month. Lastly, it gives your buyer a specific call to action. If you give people the option to pro-crastinate, you can believe they will take it. You will most definitely get the question, "when do you need the money by?" The answer is now.

Step 2: Create a list of target buyers.

Based on the Success Equation in Chapter 5, set your sales goal.

Example:

Goal Date:	90 Days
Monetary Goal:	$5,000
Retail Price:	$20
Total Book Sales:	250 Books
Monthly Book Sales:	83.3 (84)

Weekly Book Sales: 20.8   (21)
Daily Book Sales: 3

If you need to sell 250 books, look at every contact in your cell phone, in your email list, in your
high school yearbook, and in your social media
followers. Find 250 strong targets. Don't hope
for them and please don't believe posting 1 video
on Instagram is a sufficient call to action. My
brother… my literal blood brother, posts everything he does on social media, and I still find out
from other people when he is sick. You have to
contact your targets in every way.

- Voice to Voice
- Text
- Email
- Snail mail
- Social media
- Face to face

(See example of contact list on next page)

Name	Phone	Email	Mail Ad- dress	Social Media	Meet- ing	Status

Step 3: Create a Proof of Product

If you don't have a physical book, then create your book cover. You want to create a postcard or some kind of ticket that people who buy the book will get to hold. Even a small trinket is sufficient to satisfy the psychological exchange of money. It is a form of receipt that their money has been invested in a product.

If you already have your book, it's time to start increasing your promotions and keeping the book cover front and center.

Step 4: Prepare your script:

Write out your sales script, book pitch, and list of rebuttal responses. Prepare yourself to relay the value your book offers your target and also with an arsenal of words to overcome objections and procrastinators.

Step 5: Automate your purchase options:

It is very important that you remove any obstacle whatsoever. The slightest pause can lead to a missed opportunity. Create a QR code to scan that will take customers directly to the website to purchase the book if they don't have cash. Do you best to get an immediate commitment.

Obstacle: *"Okay, I don't have the cash right now."*

Solution: *"No problem. I take cashapp, paypal, credit card payments with Square"*

Step 6: Put in the Work! Execute!

Reach Each Target: Set a goal to personally reach every person on your hit list in the first 30 days. That would equate to **9 calls per day.** Call them and speak with them directly. Get a verbal commitment. Your verbal commitment means that you have been given permission to follow up.

Urgency: You want the sale TODAY. Your language should be affirmative, not passive. Do

NOT say, "Yeah, when you get a chance, if it's not too much, It would be great if…" You want to speak in the affirmative. "I really appreciate your support. How many copies would you like to buy today?"

Create a follow-up schedule. You can't afford to wait 2 weeks to follow up. Out of sight, out of mind. You need to be the squeaky wheel. You'll want to follow up every Friday. Why? Because they'll be getting paid on one of those Fridays.

Maintain communication: Remember Kevin Hart. Build your database for the future, not just for the current sale. Use this campaign as a way to initiate an ongoing relationship with your hit list targets. Use texting, email, and phone calling apps.

Create incentives to purchase early. Give people a reason to act immediately. i.e. Those who purchase early get their names in a raffle to win a prize.

Host events: Host webinars and online interviews with people who can expand your reach. Do interviews. Your hit list is just the beginning. You can still seek new targets.

Get some face time: Set up lunch dates or just pay someone a visit.

Ask ANYONE: If you have not reached your goal, then everyone you meet can help you reach it. Ask anyone you come in contact with. Adding an unexpected lead to your hit list is a win, win.

Duplicate yourself. Engage advocates who will pass out postcards, and sell books on your behalf.

Speak to Groups: Try to knock out your sales goal for the entire week or month in one session. Remember, it's a numbers game. The more people you speak to, the more opportunities you have to make a sale.

Host a Meet the Author Wine and Cheese Gathering: Mary Kay Cosmetics has created a billion dollar industry by teaching their representatives to create events with small gatherings. Do the same. Ask friends to host intimate gatherings for you to come showcase your book and get sales.

Offer a discount: If you have someone you feel is becoming a hard No, offer them a discount. Something is better than nothing. Some people appreciate a discount more than they appreciate not spending. Make the sale!

Partner with a bigger organization: There are non-profit organizations that would love to partner with you if there is a mutual benefit. Tap into larger networks.

For your consideration: Hosting an ultimate event with food and entertainment is an easy sale. When I conducted my pre-sale campaign, I sold tickets to my book release party to entice participation. $20 got you entrance into the party and your book. The place was packed. If your book has already been published, you can have a re-launch party.

This list of strategies is far from complete. Use your imagination and create opportunities. There is no guaranteed, one-size-fits-all strategy. Your goal is to create more opportunities to get more sales.

Write a letter to yourself on the
Letter to Self.

Give it to someone to mail to you on the date of
your projected goal. Utilize this as motivation
not to get the letter back unaccomplished.

Letter to Self

Dear future me!

I'm so proud of what you have accomplished. You did it! You decided that you would earn $_____ in ____months from this date_____ and you did it!

To accomplish your goal you sold:

_____ Books per month

_____ Books per week

_____ Books per day.

You adopted a professional mentality and as a result, all roads led to your desired outcome. You chose to activate your fight mode by:

_____

_____

_____

_____

You targeted your readers and generated leads by executing the following Strategies:

_____   _____

_____   _____

_____   _____

Your book pitch was as follows:

_____

_____

_____

_____

Sincerely,

Past you!

Written on _____(date)

Opened on _____ (date)

CONCLUSION

Congratulations!

You made it to the end of this book which means you're serious about turning your book into a new lucrative stream of income. I'm sure you're probably on fire and ready to take on the world. That's a great thing. Don't let that fire die. Take action quickly to move you in the direction of your goal.

If you don't know what step to take, take the easiest step. Tell someone you trust to hold you accountable. Doesn't get any easier than that. Tell them your goal. Share the dream with them, and the steps to turn the dream into a vision. Ask them to be your partner so that you can draw boldness and energy from their belief in you.

Excitement is explosive but not lasting. In order to reach your goals, you're going to need more than excitement. You're going to need strategy, focus, accountability, and help. I believe free advice is worth what you pay for it. Paying something requires commitment and leads to more engagement.

With this, I'm offering an affordable entrance fee to join the $5k Mastermind. You need to be in groups of people seeking the same goal so that you can learn from each other and push each other to greatness. $25 per month with a 6-month commitment will give you:

- Access to a network of success-driven authors
- Monthly strategy sessions
- Advice on marketing and sales strategies
- Educational resources
- Access to training from industry professionals

Find $5k Mastermind at the bottom of the page.

If you need more assistance and training, set up an appointment for more in-depth coaching.

www.ingramcontent.com/pod-product-compliance
Lightning Source LLC
Chambersburg PA
CBHW051643120626

46551CB00015B/2203

* 9 7 8 1 9 5 6 4 6 9 6 6 0 *